Live Simply – Travel Slowly – Explore Locally

THE SLOW TOURIST
Experience the exhilaration of going slow...
in
FLINTSHIRE

*For Charlie,
my Huckleberry Friend*

The Slow Tourist in Flintshire

Adventures at low speed

Sarah Lewis

© Sarah Lewis, 2019

All Rights Reserved. No part of this publication may be reproduced, stored in a retrieval system, or transmitted in any form or by any means – electronic, mechanical, photocopying, recording, or otherwise – without prior written permission from the publisher or a licence permitting restricted copying issued by the Copyright Licensing Agency, 90 Tottenham Court Road, London W1P 0LA. This book may not be lent, resold, hired out or otherwise disposed of by trade in any form of binding or cover other than that in which it is published, without the prior consent of the publisher.

Moral Rights: The author has asserted her moral right to be identified as the Author of this Work.

Published by Sigma Leisure – an imprint of
Sigma Press, Stobart House, Pontyclerc, Penybanc Road, Ammanford, Carmarthenshire SA18 3HP.

British Library Cataloguing in Publication Data
A CIP record for this book is available from the British Library.

ISBN: 978-1-910758-45-8

Typesetting and Design by: Sigma Press, Ammanford.

Cover photograph © Sarah Lewis

Photographs and drawings: © Sarah Lewis

Printed by: Akcent Media Ltd.

Disclaimer: The information in this book is given in good faith and is believed to be correct at the time of publication. No responsibility is accepted by either the author or publisher for errors or omissions, or for any loss or injury however caused. Only you can judge your own fitness, competence and experience.

Do not go where the path may lead. Go instead where there is no path and leave a trail.

Ralph Waldo Emerson

A BIT ABOUT BEING A SLOW TOURIST

Most books have a purpose, a reason why the author sat down, scratched her head, chewed her pencil and eventually began writing. The purpose of this little volume is to help you to become a SLOW TOURIST.

This is not a traditional guide book full of facts and figures, places to stay, places to eat, opening times, bus times or complicated directions. That sort of information can be found in other books and on the internet. And we won't rush around ticking off the 'must-sees' and getting exhausted either.

Instead, we'll amble to the out-of-the-way places, up alleys, behind walls, under bridges, through tunnels, down grassy lanes. We'll visit tiny museums, cosy libraries, quiet villages and hill tops; places to rest, read, ramble, write and be curious. And we'll do it AT LOW SPEED. By the end of our adventure, I hope you will have learned the art of being a slow tourist.

~~WHAT TO DO IN FLINTSHIRE~~

HOW TO <u>BE</u> IN FLINTSHIRE

BECOME A 'Slowaholic'

I happen to live in Flintshire, which is why I've begun my Slow adventure here.

I thought I knew my patch, but I've discovered places I didn't know existed, including a village called Dolphin!

I plan to write more Slow Tourist books and who knows, the next one might be about where you live. You might discover surprising places on your own doorstep and how to enjoy them, slowly

Not all who wander are lost.

H. D. Thoreau

Here are some of my favourite SLOW words and phrases

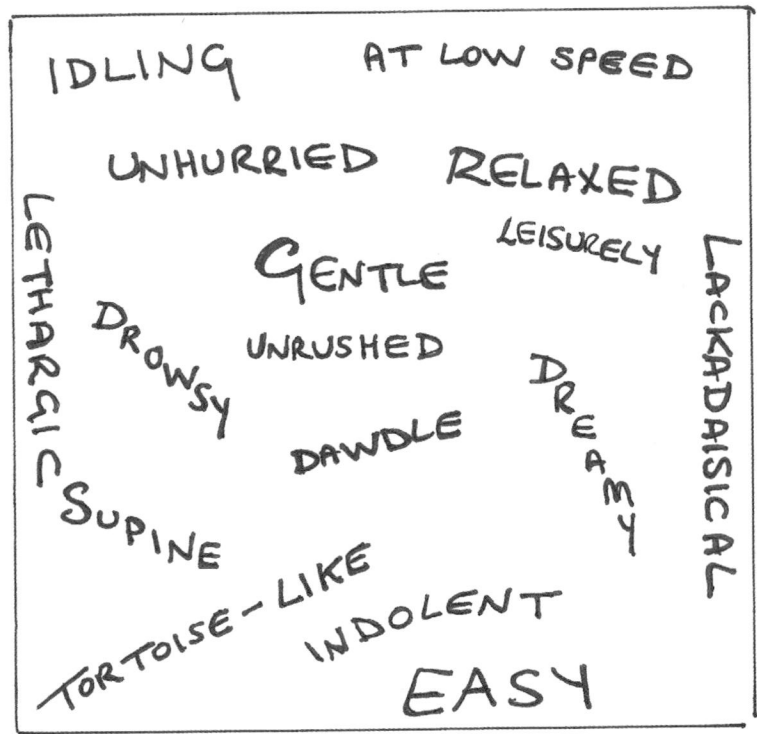

Please bear all these lovely words in mind when you are exploring.

And don't forget to travel light.

A light pouch or game bag is far less irksome, and its position may be shifted at pleasure.

Baedecker Guide to G.B. 1901

I'd like to introduce you to Sleepy Sparrow. She will accompany you on your adventure and every now and again offer you a *SloMo Suggestion*.

SloMos are Slow Moments to help you relax and enjoy your slow adventure even more.

I was always taught that it was wrong to write in books. I still can't do it. But this little book is different. You have permission to doodle, write, stick things on the pages in fact, I'd really love you to.

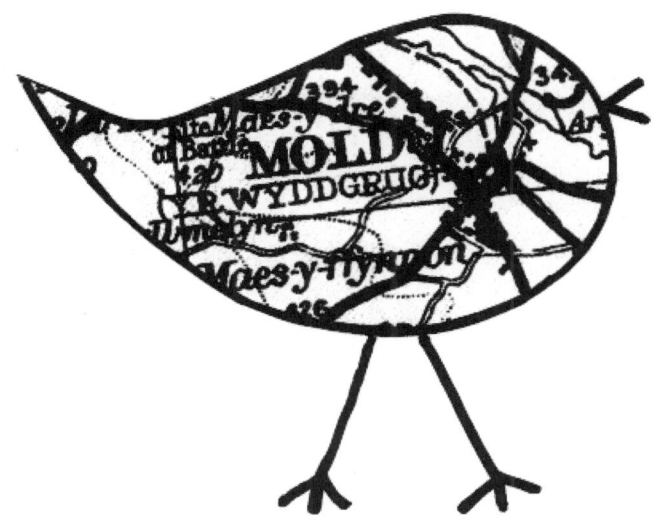

Sleepy Sparrow's advice on how to be SLOW...

WATCH

SNIFF

TOUCH

DOODLE

WONDER

WANDER

FOOT PATH

LISTEN

Your very first SloMo Suggestion

To remind you to be slow as you make your tour of Flintshire, write down the previous words on small pieces of paper, fold them and put them into a bag or pocket. During your wanderings, take one out at random.

A good traveller has no fixed plans and is not intent on arriving.
Lao Tzu

A BIT ABOUT FLINTSHIRE...

It's often called The Gateway to Wales. Gates are for coming through, opening up the way to other places, and often that's what people do, they whizz through on their way to the drama of Snowdonia or the cosy coves of Anglesey.

But gates are also for leaning on. So let's lean, have a look around and slowly explore what's on the other side, I think you'll be surprised.

Flintshire is bordered by the Irish Sea, The River Dee and the rolling Clwydian hills, an Area of Outstanding Natural Beauty. You can walk from the highest point, Moel Famau, down to the sea at Prestatyn along the Offa's Dyke footpath (21 miles/33.79km).

Much of the landscape has been shaped by its underlying geology; limestone, lead, zinc, silver and coal.

Its proximity to the coast and the industrial North of England added to its importance during the industrial revolution.

Over the years it has been home to pilgrims, Cornish tin miners, quarrymen, industrialists, explorers and poets.

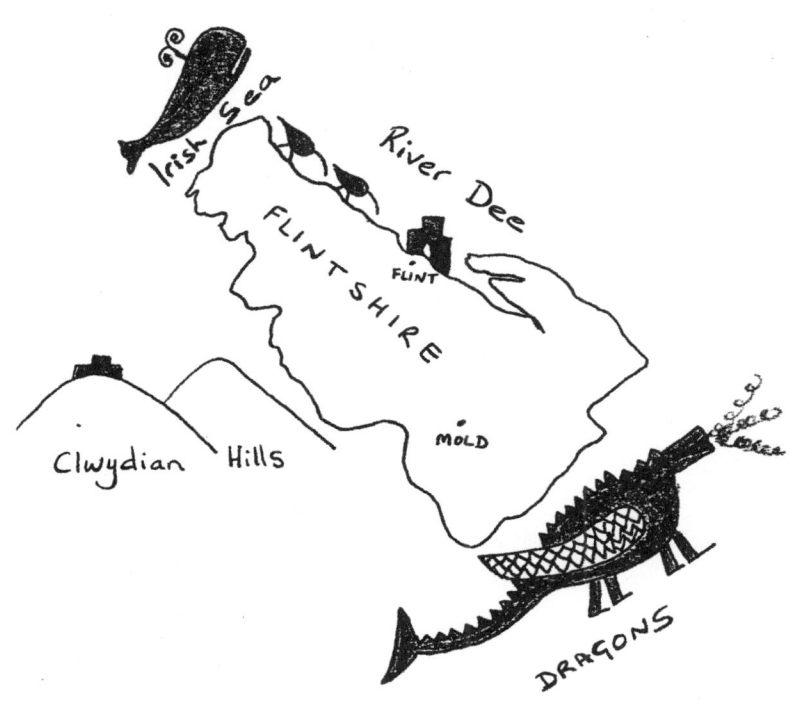

SOME SLOW FACTS ABOUT FLINTSHIRE

It's the smallest county in North Wales

It's a Fairtrade county

It has four castles

Two award winning clean beaches

Its highest point is Moel Famau – 554m

It's the driest county in Wales (Hmmm, I wonder about this fact).

It gets four mentions in *Best Wild Places in Britain and Ireland.*

BE A SLOWAHOLIC IN FLINTSHIRE AND...

sleep in a library

climb on a castle

bathe in healing waters

make a pilgrimage

begin an epic coastal walk

scamper on an iron age fortress

eat some local produce

visit an officially SLOW town.

SLOW ADVENTURES BEGIN WITH A MAP...

One of the best ways to get to know a place is to study an Ordnance Survey map. You can view them on-line but there's no substitute for the silky feel and scrunchy sound of a paper map (libraries have a good stock of them).

I like to spread a map on the living room floor and sprawl out next to it. Once you get your eye in you can read it like a good book, tracing rivers and footpaths with your fingertips. Find the contour lines, if they are very close together, the land is steep. Look for castles and strange place names, imagine how they made maps years ago without computers.

The maps that cover Flintshire are Ordnance Survey Landranger 117 and 116 and Explorer 265 and 266

If you already live in Flintshire, pretend you don't! Act like a tourist and discover new places.

I'm going to guide you to a few places I enjoy for their slow-ness but by all means, read your map and discover your own.

Gadgets are great but there's nothing quite like learning to navigate the slow way using a map and compass. (You can use your gadgets to watch a how-to video on line.) You'll feel so good when you learn to find your way around by reading a map and following the wobbly compass arrow.

For excellent advice on how to read a map, go to www.ramblers.org.uk

And for all the maps you'll ever need (you can never have enough maps) www.ordnancesurvey.co.uk

SloMo Suggestion

Make your own map.

You could make it big on a roll of lining paper and stick it on your wall. Add doodles and post cards and bus tickets to it as you explore. If you're on holiday, it's a great way to keep your memories and probably more fun than clicking through photos on your computer in years to come.

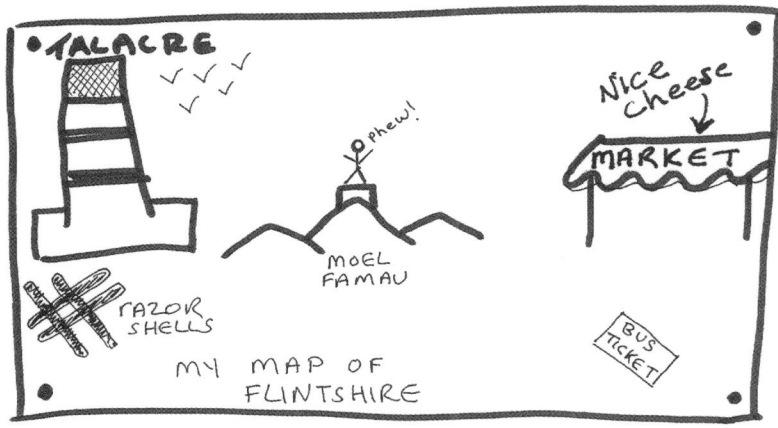

Your own map...

*It is not down in any map;
true places never are.*

Herman Melville

SloMo Suggestions

Begin a Slow Journal about your visit to Flintshire.

As well as 'what, where, when', jot down things you notice and how you feel. Use your senses to deepen your work. Don't get bogged down with detail, be light, enjoy recording your adventures.

You never know, one day it might become a bestseller or even a useful historical document?.

Travel/Nature journals to read

At the Water's Edge by John Lister-Kaye, who has taken the same circular walk from his home for the last 30 years. Each day he notices something new and records his thoughts in a journal.

An Eye on the Hebrides, by Mairi Hedderwick, a beautifully illustrated record of her six month solitary journey through the Western Isles of Scotland.

Slow sketching

Sketching and doodling is a great way to slow down and really notice what's around you.

Add doodles to your sketch book or to the blank spaces in this book. They don't have to be perfect. Have fun.

www.johnmuirlaws.com for all you need to know about nature journaling and sketching.

Not snoozing but sketching...

SLOW DOWN IN A SLOW TOWN

Believe it or not, Mold is officially a SLOW town, though you might not think so on market days (Wednesday and Saturday) when it is colourful and bustling.

It was given its SLOW status in 2006 when it became the first town in Wales to join the Cittaslow movement, 'set up in the 1990s by some laid back Italians to combat the stresses of modern life'. (www.cittaslowmold.co.uk)

It promotes local food, independent businesses and community spaces.

At the time of writing an exciting new project called Wild About Mold was being set up with plans to create a network of pedestrian friendly routes, rich in wildlife and accessible to all with community run growing areas, colourful green spaces and lots of events for people to join in with.

www.facebook.com/wildaboutmold

Mold Market has been around since 1808 and some say it's one of the best in North Wales.

On the first and third Saturday of each month there's also a farmer's market in St. Mary's Church Hall and a noisy livestock market every Friday, one of the few still located in the middle of a town. Definitely an olfactory experience!

Take some cheese from the famous Cheese Man, some homemade bread or a locally made pie and wander to the top of the High Street towards the war memorial where you'll find Bailey Hill, the remains of a Norman Motte and Bailey castle and the birthplace of Mold.

You'll also find a fine view of the Clwydian Hills and a stone circle erected in 1922 for the National Eisteddford. There are plans to transform the site with a café and amphi-theatre, but at the time of writing it is just a peaceful, tree-ful mound with a view.

If you're there on a certain date in early June, you'll find the Bailey Hill Festival in full swing, with live music, living history and storytelling at the stone circle.

www.cittaslowmold.co.uk
www.moldtowncouncil.org.uk

On the top floor of the public library in Daniel Owen Square in Mold, you will find a tiny museum crammed with fascinating objects. You can easily while away a slow hour or two here.

In a glass case is a replica of the famous 4,000 year old Mold Gold Cape, one of the WORLD'S great bronze-age treasures, the largest piece of prehistoric gold work found in Britain. It was found in a field under Bryn-yr-Ellyllon – The Hill of the Goblins, in 1833. It is featured (no. 19) in *A History of the World in 100 objects*, by Neil MacGregor.

www.britishmuseum.org

It is an amazing, sophisticated piece which also contained amber beads from the Baltic, indicating that extensive trade took place with North West Europe and the story of its discovery in the field nearby is certainly worth exploring.

You can also find out about Daniel Owen himself, 'father of the modern Welsh novel', born in Mold and described as the Welsh Charles Dickens!

If you are visiting during October, you might catch the Daniel Owen festival and find something in the programme of events to take your fancy.

www.danielowenfestival.org

SloMo Suggestion

A good way to get the feel of a place and get lost in its atmosphere is to read a book set in the locality.

Get a copy of *Enoc Huws* or *Rhys Lewis* by Daniel Owen and sit in Daniel Owen Square on a quiet day with a slice of Barabrith and a take-away panad (cup of tea) from a nearby café.

THEATRE CLWYD

One mile from Mold this theatre is, well, more than just a theatre. It's a place for community, for performance, for poetry, yoga, films, art exhibitions. It's a meeting place, an eating place, a creative place and a musical place.

If you live nearby, why not become a volunteer usher?

www.theatrclwyd.com

What did you do in Mold? What surprised you?

Use this page to make a list.

There are a lot of great places to eat in and around Mold. I'm not going to single any out in this little book but your SLOW challenge is to eat something that you've never eaten before.

What did you eat?

Describe it using your five senses – sight, sound, smell, taste, touch. You might struggle to find a sound to describe your new food! Perhaps there was a sound when you cut into it, or took a bite, or when it was cooking?

Visit www.foodtrail.co.uk for details of the Clwydian Range food trail.

Food senses...

Doodle your new food here...

> He was a bold man that first ate an oyster.

Johnathan Swift

SLOW ART
Earth without ART is just Eh.
Anonymous

Taking the time to study a painting is a great slow thing to do, as is watching an artist.

Flintshire has a thriving artist community. There are regular exhibitions at Theatre Clwyd.

Visit www.fvacn.org.uk, the web site of Flintshire Visual Arts and Crafts Network to find out about local artists and what's on. There might be a workshop you can join on your visit.

Each September the Helfa Gelf Art Trail takes place across North Wales with over 400 artists studios open to the public, many of which are in Flintshire. Pick up the little Helfa Gelf booklet and choose the studios you'd like to visit. It's a great opportunity to meet the artists and find out how they do what they do. You never know, you may be inspired to have a go yourself. Some studios are in sheds at the bottom of gardens, some in houses, some in church halls, some artists get together and demonstrate their art as a group. Many of them even offer tea and cake! All offer a warm welcome.

www.helfagelf.co.uk

Andy Goldsworthy is an environmental artist who has been making art out in nature for decades now. Tim Pugh is local to this area and does a similar thing.

Why not have a go yourself?

SloMo Suggestion

At the beach, in the woods or in the park, without damaging anything of course, make a collage with fallen leaves, shells, pebbles or sand. Or build a simple shape with twigs or stones.

Sketch or photograph your art and then leave it for nature to play with or for someone else to find and enjoy. Share your pictures on the internet or print them off and add them to your Slow Journal.

BOOK SOME SLOW TIME

Libraries are great places to be SLOW in.

Flintshire has a very special one – Gladstone's Library, in the village of Hawarden.

www.gladstoneslibrary.co.uk

It was founded by William Gladstone, four times Prime Minister of Great Britain. You can sleep there, dream there, eat fabulous food there, warm your feet by the fire there, play chess there and yes, you can also read there. If you call in around 12pm, 2pm or 4pm you can go on a mini guided tour and step into the silent and beautiful Hogwarty reading room. In 2015 it was voted best wellbeing retreat by readers of *The Guardian*.

They hold regular craft fairs, literary events, talks and workshops.

Provide them with a bit of info and you can become a reader there with access to a secluded desk, lamp and the opportunity to visit when you like and write or read or simply watch the dust motes glide in the beams of light coming through the leaded windows, which is often what I end up doing. Well, it is such a slow place.

I cannot remember the books I've read any more than the meals I have eaten; even so, they have made me.

Ralph Waldo Emerson

STOP!

Are you being SLOW enough?

ALSO IN HAWARDEN

More Slow things to do while you are in Hawarden
(sounds like Harden. In Welsh it is Penarlag)

Pick your own fruit on Hawarden Estate.
www.hawardenestate.co.uk

Go to a festival that celebrates the great outdoors.
www.thegoodlifeexperience.co.uk

Go through the big red gates in the centre of the village and stroll in the woodland in the grounds of the ruined 13th century castle. The 'new' castle is owned by the Gladstone/Glynne family who still live there.

SLOW SECRETS

Rhydymwyn is a small village with a big history.

It's quite hard to say Rhydymwyn let alone find its secret valley Nature Reserve. Enemy aircraft during World War Two didn't find it but Michael Portillo has been there, so has Prof Brian Cox and Welsh naturalist Iolo Williams. If you follow the A541 towards Denbigh out of Mold, three miles along you will find the village. Turn left into Nant Alyn Road and look for the big green railings.

It wasn't always a nature reserve. During the war years, this site was so secret it wasn't named on any maps. Once known as the X Site, now it's home to great crested newts, bats, bee orchids, otters, green woodpeckers, redstarts and many more species. It remains a closed site, which adds to its peaceful charm but if you telephone 01352 741 591 you can arrange to visit. There are regular events and art workshops there and if you live not far away, you might consider becoming a member of Friends of Rhydymwyn Valley for £5 and then you can visit the site as often as you like.

www.facebook.com/friendsofrhydymwynvalley

Rhydymwyn means ford of the ore. There were lots of lead mines in the area. The Leete watercourse was constructed in 1823 to drive the water wheels that pumped excess water from the mines. It is now a dry trail which you can now follow all the way to Loggerheads Country Park and café.

Charles Kingsley who wrote *The Water Babies* frequently walked along the Leete.

The famous mining engineer and entrepreneur John Taylor rented nearby Coed Du Hall and in 1829 the composer Felix Mendelssohn broke his journey through Wales to stay with the Taylors at the Hall. Whilst there, he composed *The Rivulet*, inspired by the River Alyn.

There is a plaque mentioning Mendlessohn and Kingsley on the wall opposite the entrance to Rhydymwyn Nature Reserve in Nant Alyn Road.

SloMo Suggestions

Think like a composer or a writer. Listen to the sounds around you, if the river is running (it vanishes into swallow holes in the limestone river bed at times of low rainfall and comes up again near Loggerheads Country Park), listen to its gurgle. Hear the wind in the tall trees, and the bird song. Imagine being inspired by these sounds to write a piece of music, what instruments would you use to recall these sounds?

Charles Kingsley wrote *The Water Babies*. Could you begin a tale inspired by the river and the woods? If the river is dry, perhaps there's a reason why? Maybe a great, grumpy Red Dragon has swallowed all the water and the local people have to find the bravest person to go and ask him to spit it out again so they can hold their annual duck race!

In fact, the fairies had turned him into a water baby. A water baby? You never heard of a water baby. Perhaps not. That is the very reason why this story was written.

Charles Kingsley

My story notes...

FLINT

is a town on the coast. It's a place of arrivals and departures. In winter, thousands of birds arrive to feed on the rich, oozy mud of the Dee Estuary. The watery winter sun turns the mud silver and the twisting and turning of thousands of wading birds is mesmerizing.

The lovely crumbly castle at the water's edge is a fine place for listening to the call of curlew, oystercatchers and redshank. It was the first in the chain of castles in North Wales built by Edward I.

From here you can join the North Wales Coast Path and make your way, slowly, all around the coastline of Wales. If you come back up the Offa's Dyke path, you will have circumnavigated Wales!

www.northwalescoastpath.co.uk

Flint also has a railway station where you can catch the train all the way to Holyhead, or even to London.

Did you see the giant foot?

Never look back unless you are planning to go that way.

H. D. Thoreau

SloMo Suggestion

I love to see how birdsongs are described and spelled in bird guides.

My RSPB guide describes the following:

Black-tailed godwit – weeka-weeka-weeka

Oystercatcher – kleep kleep kleep

Magpie – chacker, chacker, chacker

Black-headed gull – kree-aaa

Redshank – tew tew tew.

Starlings mimic the calls and songs of other birds. I was once baffled as to why I heard a curlew in a strange place, turned out to be a starling doing a very good impression!

Close your eyes and listen. How would you spell the sounds you hear? Write them here or in your Slow Journal.

Do you have a favourite bird? Describe its song. Why is it your favourite? Write about it here or in your journal.

SLOW HISTORY

There are quite a few Iron Age Hillforts in and around Flintshire. My favourite is Moel y Gaer, a friendly mound near Rhosesmor and Halkyn. It's a fairly easy walk, nearly always quiet and you can see for miles and miles, across the Dee and the Mersey, the Two Liverpool Cathedrals and beyond to the hills of Lancashire and Cumbria. With binoculars, you can even see Blackpool Tower on a clear day!

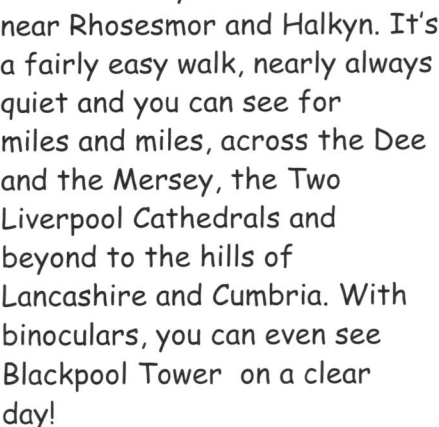

The hill fort is a great place to come on New Year's Eve. At midnight, thousands of tiny explosions fizz in the darkness below.

I like to imagine how it must have been up here 2,500 years ago. Well, I wouldn't have seen Blackpool Tower then, but what would I have seen?

SloMo Suggestion

Sit on the soft grass around the ramparts, imagine what you would have seen 2,500 years ago ... sheep, men chipping stone, chopping wood? What can you see from here now?

When you get home, look up The Iron Age and see how they lived.

Or visit www.heatherandhillforts.co.uk

List what you can see...

From here you can explore the many paths that criss-cross the common land towards Rhes-y-cae and Halkyn ...

HALKYN

www.halkynmountain.co.uk

While you're walking around, you might notice how lumpy the ground is. People have mined here since the Roman times. This area was once one of the largest producers of lead in the whole of Britain. In the spring, look out for a plant like a carpet of white stars. The presence of spring sandwort or leadwort was used by miners as an indicator of a lead vein beneath the surface. You can find more evidence of mining by looking for shaft craters (conical depressions in the ground) and tips (mounds of waste rock). I love the strange concrete bee-hive structures that pepper the rough ground, these are capped mine shafts, sealed in the 1980s. Some have slots in to accommodate the local bats.

Beneath Halkyn Mountain there's a vast network of over 62 miles of tunnels!

Amble around and take in the big views, towards the Irish Sea and Snowdonia, Lancashire and Cumbria.

There are information boards dotted around this wide open landscape to tell you more about mining, quarrying, underground tunnels and the mountain communities of miners, quarrymen and farmers. In 1858, Halkyn had two blacksmiths, two cobblers, a butcher, three grocery and general shops, one tailor and a drapery, as well as seven taverns.

*Adopt the pace of nature.
Her secret is patience.*
Ralph Waldo Emerson

Over Halkyn and Brynford common land and on towards Holywell is another place that positively invites you to be SLOW – Pantasaph Friary.

It's been there for over 125 years but I've only recently discovered it whilst on a bike ride. St. Pio's café is snuggled inside a sunny courtyard amongst the extensive Friary buildings and the welcome you receive instantly makes you want to relax , pick up a magazine, order an extremely creamy cappuccino and not go anywhere for an hour or so. There are gardens to roam in and a beautiful church to explore. It's a place of contemplation, companionship, cake and cappuccino!

Ask me for a certain number of dollars if you will, but do not ask me for my afternoons.
Henry David Thoreau

HOLYWELL – 'THE LOURDES OF WALES'

This small town is named after the well at the shrine of St. Winefride, one of the Seven Wonders of Wales. The story goes that back in the 7th Century, Winefride refused the advances of Prince Caradoc, who cut off her head in anger. The head rolled down hill and where it lay, a spring started. Fortunately, she was restored to life by her Uncle, St. Beuno. The well is believed to have healing properties and pilgrims have visited ever since. You can arrange to take a dip yourself if you fancy it.

www.saintwinefrideswell.com

SloMo Suggestion

To immerse yourself in the soul of the place without taking a dip in the waters, sit in the grounds and read the Brother Cadfael story, *A Morbid Taste for Bones* by Ellis Peters, a tale about the removal of St Winefred's body to Shrewsbury Abbey.

What are the other six wonders of Wales?

List them here.

*Life is a journey,
not a destination.*
Ralph Waldo Emerson

GREENFIELD VALLEY HERITAGE PARK

www.greenfieldvalley.com

Described as, 'the cradle of the industrial revolution in North Wales, where goods were made and shipped all over the world', SLOW is not a word you would have associated this area with once upon a time. But now, amongst all the monuments and ruins and preserved buildings that tell its bustling, noisy, fascinating history, it is has a lot to offer us SLOW visitors.

The Heritage Park is a 1.5 mile linear park following the Holywell Stream from below the town out towards the River Dee coast. Now, the valley is filled with birdsong, the sound of water and children playing and one of the fastest things you might see these days is a kingfisher zooming down the Stream! It's hard to imagine that this was once a bustling, noisy, dirty valley with a narrow gauge railway, mills, forges, farms and other buildings to do with the trade in cotton, copper and brass.

At the end of the valley are the peaceful ruins of Basingwerk Abbey, once the home of Cistercian Monks, dating from 1132.

The ruins are lovely to wander amongst on a summery day.

SloMo Suggestion

Composing poetry is a SLOW thing to do and helps you notice what's around you.

My favourite is the haiku, an ancient Japanese form of poetry that consists of three lines with five syllables in the first line, seven in the second and five in the third. They are often about nature and seasons and are like a little snap shot, capturing a fleeting moment in time.

As you walk along the path through this Heritage Park, think about the valley then and now, make some notes and have a go at writing a sequence of Haiku. You could send them in to the visitor centre.

Haiku

Snapshots from my bike
golden pheasant gliding low
geese in formation

Dull brown sparrow –
where it bathed in snow,
a tiny angel shape.

Ten goldfinches bounce
across a water-wash sky,
tinkling ice chimes.

Prints in powder snow
blackbird, badger, rabbit, fox
yours, mine – heading home.

Poems/Words/Thoughts

MORE IN HOLYWELL

Walkers are Welcome (especially SLOW ones). Look for the yellow circle with the walking boot footprints inside.

www.holywellwalkersarewelcome.org

You can follow several local trails as well as nearby long distance footpaths;

Wat's Dyke Way – 61 miles
www.watsdykeway.org

North Wales Pilgrim's Way – 134 miles
www.pilgrims-way-north-wales.org

All Wales Coast Path – opened in 2012 and voted by Lonely Planet as one of the World's top destinations in 2015.
www.walescoastpath.gov.uk

World famous naturalists, explorers and wanderers Thomas Pennant and Henry Morton Stanley lived nearby.

www.cymdeithasthomaspennant.com has several walks associated with Thomas Pennant. In the nearby Greenfield Valley Heritage Park, there is a museum dedicated to his life.

Amongst other things, Stanley searched for the source of the Nile.

The walker and naturalist does not wear a hat, or a shoe, or a coat to be looked at but for other uses.
Henry David Thoreau

SloMo Suggestion

 It's not quite the Nile but follow the Holywell Stream along the Greenfield Valley as far as Greenfield Dock, where Pilgrims once came ashore to visit St. Winefride's Well.

Now the Dock is peaceful, local boats lie in the soft mud and it is another place where you can pick up the coastal path either way, towards Chester or Bangor. There are views across the Dee towards Parkgate.

The journey of 1000 miles must begin with a single step.
Lao Tzu

SloMo Suggestion

Visit the Thomas Pennant museum then follow his example and go on your own journey, or perhaps take one of the walks described on the website. Take your notebook and write down what you see, who you meet.

Describe and draw plants and animals, press leaves between the pages, stick them into your notebook when they are dry.

What is the most fascinating fact you found out?
What surprised you?
What amazed you?
What do you want to find out more about?

SLOW LEGENDS

I like legends. There are a few great ones in Flintshire.

Gop Hill Cairn is on a high hill overlooking Trelawnydd, near Prestatyn. It's the second largest Neolithic mound in Britain, smaller only than Silbury Hill. Legend has it that it was the site of Queen Boudicca's last battle against the Romans and there are those who claim she rides her chariot through the lanes at night. Whatever ghosts wander about up there, on a clear sunny day there are fabulous views and a lovely circular walk that can be found in the Rural Walks in Flintshire booklet from www.flintshire.gov.uk.

Carreg Carn March Arthur – The Stone of the hoof of Arthur's Horse. There is an old parish boundary stone near the village of Cadole, near Loggerheads (Map Ref: SJ202626). Legend has it that the stone bears the hoofprint of King Arthur's horse as he leapt from a nearby cliff (some say the summit of Moel Famau) to escape the invading Saxons.

Maes Garmon monument. (Map Ref: SJ22256469) A stone obelisk set up in a field near Mold in 1736 to commemorate the Alleluia battle and the victory of the Britons over the Saxons in AD 420. Apparently the Christian Britons shouted 'Alleluia' three times before the battle. The sound amplified in the surrounding hills causing the larger Saxon 'heathen' forces to panic and run.

The battle was recorded by Bede and even though there is no evidence that it took place here, it's a nice obelisk and worth a slow look.

Talacre Lighthouse. There are those who claim to have seen a ghostly lighthouse keeper in old fashioned clothes standing on the balcony in front of the glass dome.

Flint Castle. Ravens nest in the castle ruins. One of my favourite legends is about two Ravens called Huginn and Muninn. Each morning they set off at dawn to fly around the world and at dinner they returned to the Norse God Odin with all the information about what they'd seen and heard.

Listen to the call of a raven. Their heavy 'kronk, kronk' seems to fall from the sky like a nugget of iron ore. In spring they tumble through the air together in a lovely skydance.

SloMo Suggestion

Make up your own legend. Be as fanciful as you like. You could have flying horses, magic wells, secret caverns. Flintshire is full of wells, springs, mines, caverns, hills, fortresses. Read as much as you can about the area and see if you could turn any of the facts into great legends.

www.wellhopper.wordpress.com

Jot down some ideas here...

> Write it on your heart that every day is the best day in the year.
> R. W. Emerson

SLOW SEASHORE

Follow Flintshire's boundary with the River Dee towards its mouth, turn the corner and gasp at the big sky and the endless stretch of sand at Talacre, a great place to practice being slow.

The dunes behind the beach are a Site of Special Scientific Interest and home to rare natterjack toads and sand lizards. Listen out for stonechats, making a sound like two pebbles being tapped together. Watch out for the reed bunting, looking like a country parson delivering his sweet sermon from the top of the scrubby bushes.

The striking lighthouse is another place of legend. Numerous reports of the ghostly figure of a lighthouse keeper standing on the balcony inspired artist Angela Smith to create the 7ft metallic sculpture who now stands at the rails. It can look quite spooky when there's a fog creeping in from the sea and gulls screeching overhead.

Further along the coastal path is Gronant, not strictly in Flintshire, but if you visit in the summer, it is well worth crossing the invisible boundary into Denbighshire.

Stroll along the boardwalk, past clumps of silver-blue sea holly and spikes of pink orchids towards the sea and you will hear a most energetic, not at all slow sound. Look up when you hear that sound, like lots of creaking gate hinges, and you'll see rare little terns, chasing and wheeling, like miniature masked avengers. These feisty little birds come here to nest every year, all the way from West Africa. Despite the caravans and walkers, the birds of prey and storms, they manage to raise their chicks before heading back to Africa in early August. The birds are watched over by a whole team of dedicated wardens and volunteers. If you are on holiday, you might even volunteer yourself (contact the Denbighshire Countryside Service). Spending time in this great big space is a real treat.

www.denbighshirecountryside.org.uk

SloMo Suggestion

Beach Art

There are often lots of razor shells along the beach at Talacre. Collect some and make shapes, flowers, fish, birds, spirals. Photograph them for your journal/map. What do you know about razor shells? Would you find them on rocky coasts?

Find out about them from a book or the internet. *Collin's Complete Guide to British Coastal Wildlife* is a great book.

SloMo Suggestions

 Razor shells are washed up after storms and a lot of them together are sometimes called a wreck. Collective nouns are fun, for example; a murder of crows, a parliament of owls, a school of dolphins, an army of caterpillars.

Look around you for groups of things – pebbles, sand, people, children, clouds, bees, birds and make up some collective nouns for them. For example; a crashing of pebbles, a shave of razor shells, a screeching of gulls.

Snooze on the sand. Listen to the waves, the gulls, the wind in the marram grass. Make sure you wear plenty of sun cream though.

Don't forget to sketch what you see at the beach. Focus in on the patterns in shells, leaves and driftwood. Drawing helps you slow down and really see the world. Your sketches don't have to be perfect, just have fun and be SLOW.

My thoughts from the seaside...

*The world is big
and I want to get a good look
at it before dark.*
John Muir

SLOW PARK

Local parks are great places to explore and often overlooked by tourists. Flintshire has Wepre Park, a peaceful 160 acres in busy Connah's Quay, with a visitor centre and café.

www.flintshire.gov.uk

The woods are the last remnants of the great hunting forest of Ewloe and in the past would have been filled with the sound of fighting and arrows and guns. Thankfully the sounds you are more likely to hear in the woods are bright birdsong and bubbling Wepre Brook. There are great crested newts, bats and badgers. You might see the blue flash of a Kingfisher or the white bib of a dipper 'dipping' from a rock in the middle of the brook.

Once you've strolled through the ancient woods, it's very exciting to come upon the crumbly remains of the 12th century Ewloe Castle, a great place for a picnic.

The question is not what you look at, but what you see.

H.D. Thoreau

SloMo Suggestion

Slow Sounds

Sit on a log and listen. Wepre woods is an ancient place. Imagine the sounds you might have heard in the 12th century – wild pigs, arrows being fired, the shouts of men in battle?

What can you hear now, children playing, distant traffic?

Listen beyond these sounds, let your ears tune in to insects, water, the clatter of bird's wings overhead, the crisp rustle of leaves, the soft whistle of wind in grasses, rain drops on the surface of a pond.

I hear...

Can you identify any of the bird songs? (*Bird Watching with your Eyes Closed* by Simon Barnes may help.)

Robin

List the bird songs you can hear...

SLOW WOODLAND

In the village of Hendre, four miles north-west of Mold on the A541, is a delightful little patch of ancient woodland called Coed y Felin.

The best time to visit is spring, when it is filled with bluebells. If you look ahead as you walk on the woodland path, you will see a haze of blue under the new, lime green leaves of beech trees. Their perfume is sweet and rich enough to make you giddy!

If you are lucky you will see and hear a dapper little black and white bird called a pied flycatcher. They return here every year from West Africa to make good use of the many bird boxes put up by the North Wales Wildlife Trust, who manage this reserve.

www.northwaleswildlifetrust.org.uk

Look up Pied Flycatchers and listen to their song on this website: www.rspb.co.uk

> What business have
> I in the woods,
> if I am thinking
> of something
> out of the woods?

Henry David Thoreau

SloMo Suggestion

Blooming Marvellous!

Apart from bluebells, Coed y Felin has wood anemones, celandines, primroses, wild garlic and on the limestone slopes, orchids.

Get right down and really look at the tiny flowers, how many petals have they got? What's the very centre of the flower like? What shape are the leaves? In your Slow Journal, Doodle some of the flowers you find, or photograph them and find out their names when you get home.

Which is your favourite flower?

Why?

William Wordsworth composed a famous poem about daffodils. Could you write one about bluebells? Think about their shape, their perfume, the insects who visit them, the sort of trees they grow under, how they make you feel.

Or sketch them with a blue water-colour pencil or some soft pastel crayons. Or just sit and sniff and listen for the song of the pied flycatcher and think of the long journey it has made just to be here in these Welsh woods.

Notes and doodles...

Another special woodland is The Warren near Bodfari.

Here, at the Woodland Skills Centre, you can really learn to slow down by practicing Mindfulness in the Woods, learning to weave willow, make a chair or hone your bush craft skills. At their lovely family events you can all slow down together. There's music in the woods, you can even make your very own coracle! Is there a slower mode of transport? It's a fab place with a lovely ethos and community spirit and a warm welcome.

www.woodlandskillscentre.uk

SLOW SHOWS

County and village shows are great local events where you can spend a few slow hours.

Cilcain is a pretty village at the base of Moel Famau. It has a fascinating church, a cosy pub, a fabulous and friendly village shop and a legendary Village Show each August Bank Holiday.

At the show, there's Punch and Judy, dog obedience (which often turns into dog disobedience), home grown produce tent, tea tent with harpist and home-made cakes and the famous Mountain Race where competitors run up and down Moel Famau as fast as they can (not for us slow tourists that one). But, the highlight has to be Teddy Bear Parachuting. Bears are attached to tiny parachutes and launched off the church tower, to the delight and dismay (when a treasured bear becomes entangled in a tree or strikes the brickwork on the way down) of the crowd below. Don't worry, none are harmed and they all get a certificate of bravery afterwards.

www.cilcainshow.org.uk

Rhes y Cae Horse Show has been taking place each July for well over 60 years.

Apart from horses, it has sheepdog trials and terrier racing. Terriers and Border Collies are not known for being SLOW so you might need to relax a bit after watching these.

At the time of writing, the Caerwys Village show, which happens in July, had some ideal SLOW activities you could join in with – under the 'craft' heading you could enter a 'mood board', a good idea for a slow project. And under the photography section there was a section called 'raindrops.' What an opportunity to slow down and celebrate raindrops!

www.caerwys-show.org.uk

SloMo Suggestion

Become part of the place you are visiting and join in with the village show. Enter some jam, a cake, a photo or piece of artwork. Most of them have web sites or Facebook pages with categories and dates for submissions.

More Suggestions for Slow Adventures

Head to the bus station, jump on a random bus, who knows what slow adventures you might have?

Look at postcards in shops, these can be a good way to decide what places to visit and you can send one to yourself or use it to stick on your home-made map or in your Slow Journal.

Collect tourist attraction leaflets. Cut and paste images from them onto your map or in your journal, get creative and make a collage with paints and postcards.

If you want a posh reminder of your slow adventure, take lots of photos and make a photo book or calendar on-line.

If it's raining and grey, visit the local library and have an epic adventure without getting wet, you could even go further afield - to the moon, to Everest, swim with sharks, walk with dinosaurs!

Stay in a local B&B rather than an hotel. Try and find a quirky one, on a farm or in a lighthouse, an old mill, cosy pub or in a library. www.gladstoneslibrary.co.uk

Try a spot of geocaching … www.geocaching.com

Pick up a copy of the yellow National Open Garden Scheme book and visit gardens in the area, some serve tea and cake, some have music, they all have lovely flowers to wander amongst. There a quite a few entries for Flintshire.

www.ngs.org.uk

HELPFUL PAGES
Some Books You Might Enjoy

The Peregrine by J.A. Baker

At The Water's Edge – A Walk in the Wild by John Lister Kaye

Walden and other writings of Henry David Thoreau

The poems of Simon Armitage and Billy Collins

How to Draw Anything by Mark Linley

Bradt Travel Guides – *Bus Pass Britain – 50 of the nations favourite Bus journeys*

The Idle Traveller by Dan Kieran

The Natural Navigator by Tristan Gooley

Wild Places by Robert MacFarlane

A Book of Silence by Sara Maitland

How to be a Bad Birdwatcher by Simon Barnes

Bird Watching with your Eyes Closed by Simon Barnes

A Sand County Almanac by Aldo Leopold

Idle Thoughts by Jerome K Jerome

Food for Free by Richard Mabey

Enoc Huws, Rhys Lewis – books by Welsh author, Daniel Owen

On Writing by Stephen King

An Eye on the Hebrides: An illustrated journey by Mairi Crawford Hedderwick

Map Addict by Mike Parker

Lots of unusual guide books available at www.sigmapress.co.uk

SloMo Suggestion

Become a Bibliophile

As well as your journal, pen, camera, sound recorder, snacks, take a good book on your Slow adventures.

Or

Write the book you want to read!

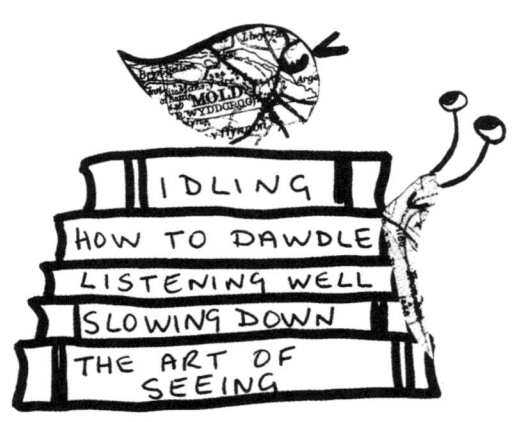

Make a list of your own favourite books, including those books you've always meant to read but haven't yet made the time for.

*Wherever you go,
go with all your heart.*

Confucius

USEFUL WEB SITES

www.visitflintshire.co.uk

www.visitwales.com

www.johnmuirlaws.com - a fantastic web site for drawing tutorials and nature journaling.

www.cittaslow.org.uk (for slow towns)

www.geocaching.com

www.ordnancesurvey.co.uk

www.ngs.org.uk - National Garden Scheme

www.rspb.org.uk

www.wildlifetrusts.org

www.rhs.org.uk - Royal Horticultural Society

www.canalrivertrust.org.uk - Canal and River Trust

www.findalibrary.org.uk

www.poetryarchive.org

www.deeestuary.co.uk - bird watching information and access to the Dee.

www.pilgrims-way-north-wales.org

www.offasdyke.org.uk

www.watsdykeway.com

www.walescoastpath.gov.uk

www.holywellwalkersarewelcome.org

www.ridenorthwales.co.uk - for biking routes

www.ebikehirenorthwales.co.uk

www.fvacn.org.uk - for all things art related in Flintshire

www.orielbodfarigallery.co.uk - a delightful gallery in the foothills of the Clwydian hills

www.helfagelf.co.uk - a month long art trail during September. Many Flintshire artists take part.

www.foodtrail.co.uk

SPECIAL SLOW DAYS

World Book Day early in March www.worldbookday.com

World Sparrow Day 20 March www.natureforever.org

Earth Hour 28 March www.earthhour.org
Join in with the rest of the world and switch off your lights for one hour

World Wildlife Day 3 March www.wildlifeday.org

International Dawn Chorus Day 1 May

Try www.northwaleswildlifetrust.org.uk for walks to join

Volunteers Week 1-7 June

World Oceans Day 8 June

International Day of Peace 21 September

National Poetry Day 7 October

Add your own

SOME FAMOUS PEOPLE ASSOCIATED WITH FLINTSHIRE

Felix Mendlessohn
Charles Kingsley
John Taylor
Henry Morton Stanley
St Winefride
Thomas Pennant
Daniel Owen
Boudica
W.E. Gladstone
King Arthur

And, now that you have discovered Slow Flintshire, written about your findings in this book and in your journal and make a map, you can add *your* name to the list!

ME!

Did you discover any other famous Flintshire people? Write their names here:

Final SloMo Suggestion

Make a SLOW Adventures Box – using an old biscuit or sweet tin or a shoe box. Put in all the things you collect on your SLOW adventure – bus/train tickets, museum/gallery entrance tickets, theatre/cinema tickets, postcards, pressed leaves, photos, doodles, leaflets, shells, pebbles, etc.

At the end of the year, when it's cold and wet outside, take out your box and re-live your adventure, slowly, with a nice cuppa and a slice of cake.

Then, plan your next SLOW Trip ...

Add your own SloMo Suggestions...

Thank you for reading this little book. I hope you've enjoyed exploring Flintshire slowly and learned a bit about the art of being a Slow Tourist.

I'd love to hear about your adventures. Did you find any other SLOW places in Flintshire?

Let me know: sleepysparrow@yahoo.co.uk

Or contact my website: www.theslowtourist.weebly.com

*Wisely and slow.
They stumble that run fast.*

William Shakespeare

THIS IS TO CERTIFY THAT

----

*HAS TRAVELLED SLOWLY IN FLINTSHIRE
AND IS OFFICIALLY*

A SLOW TOURIST